States' Rights

LEARNING RESOURCES CENTER
UNIVERSITY OF WYOMING LIBRARIES
LARAMIE, WY 82071

WITHDRAWN

DATE DUE			
FEB 26 2001			
OCT 25 2002			
JUN 13 2005			
FEB 13 2014			

HIGHSMITH 45-220

John E. Batchelor

STATES' RIGHTS

Richard B. Morris, Consulting Editor

Franklin Watts   1986   A First Book
New York   London   Toronto   Sydney

Photographs courtesy of: The Bettman Archive:
pp. 2, 8, 11, 26, 31, 34, 37, 42, 47, 51, 52, 55;
Free Library of Philadelphia: p. 14;
The New York Historical Society, New York City: p. 17.

Library of Congress Cataloging in Publication Data
Batchelor, John E.
States' rights.

(A First book)
Bibliography: p.
Includes index.
Summary: Discusses the issue of states' rights and traces the history of conflicts between states' legislatures and a strong central government from the time of the Constitutional Convention to the present day.
1. State rights—History—Juvenile literature.
[1. State rights—History] I. Title.
JK311.B37   1986   321.02'3'0973   86-1605
ISBN 0-531-10112-6

Copyright © 1986 by John E. Batchelor
Printed in the United States of America
All rights reserved
6 5 4 3 2 1

Contents

Chapter One
A Continuing Problem
1

Chapter Two
The Revolutionary Era
6

Chapter Three
The Constitution
13

Chapter Four
The Age of Jefferson
21

Chapter Five
Civil War
29

Chapter Six
Reconstruction
39

Chapter Seven
States' Rights Through the 1930s
45

Chapter Eight
States' Rights From the
1930s to Today
54

For Further Reading
61

Index
63

States' Rights

Chapter 1

A Continuing Problem

The year was 1830. The event was a celebration of the Democratic Party's good fortunes. Andrew Jackson, a Democrat, had been elected president of the United States in 1828. Several courses of dinner had been served, and the time had come to raise glasses in a toast. President Jackson stood up and glared into the eyes of his vice-president, John C. Calhoun.

"Our Union," Jackson announced. "It must be preserved."

A chill ran through the room. Out of duty to the president, every man stood and lifted his glass. Then all eyes shifted to the vice-president.

Calhoun's hand trembled. He spilled a few drops. Onlookers thought for a moment that the contents of the glass might be thrown out. But, his eyes blazing with fury, John C. Calhoun took a sip.

Could Calhoun be giving in?

Then Calhoun raised his own glass. Again, a hush fell around the room.

Calhoun's voice bore a bitter tone. "The Union. Next to our liberties, most dear."

Vice-president under both John Quincy Adams and Andrew Jackson, John C. Calhoun was a strong supporter of states' rights.

Jackson and Calhoun had not always been at odds. In fact, they had been political friends in earlier years. Both were southerners: Jackson was from Tennessee, Calhoun from South Carolina. Their split had developed over states' rights.

In 1828, Congress had passed a tariff law. A tariff is a tax on imported goods. The purpose of the tariff was to protect American manufacturers. Of course, the tariff would provide income for the federal government, too. But adding the tariff to the price of the imported goods raised the price American buyers had to pay. This made American goods cheaper than imports, but manufactured goods in general became more expensive than they would have been without the tariff.

Most American manufacturers were located in the northern states. Southerners resented having to pay higher prices in order to protect their northern neighbors. The two sections were already angry at each other over the issue of slavery. The tariff thus added fuel to their anger.

That was why Jackson and Calhoun were so angry. Although a southerner himself, Jackson believed it was his duty as president to enforce federal laws. He intended to make southerners pay the tariff, whether they liked it or not. Calhoun, loyal to his state of South Carolina, was furious in his opposition to what the South called "the tariff of abominations."

Congress passed another tariff act in 1832. The new tariff removed most of the objectionable features of the "abominations" tariff and lowered general duties slightly below those of 1824.

To the residents of South Carolina, retaining the protective principle was unsatisfactory. They elected delegates to a state convention that would deal with the tariff question. South Carolinians believed that the states had created the federal government, and therefore states had the right to nullify a federal law. "To nullify" means to declare a law void, or no longer in effect.

The South Carolina convention passed a resolution declaring the tariff laws of 1828 and 1832 nullified within the state. President Jackson grew even angrier. Federal laws applied to all the people of the United States, he argued. No state had any right to nullify a federal law. In December 1832, Jackson issued a proclamation against the nullifiers, and in March, Congress gave him additional legislation to enable him to enforce the tariff law. Trouble was avoided, however, when Congress at the same time revised the tariff, gradually reducing it.

Although this incident passed, the basic issue remained. Could states nullify federal laws? Whose authority was superior, the states' or the federal government's?

The year was 1957. The atmosphere in Little Rock, Arkansas, was tense. Armed soldiers faced each other. But these were not the forces of a foreign army. These people were all Americans.

For generations, the public schools of the South had been racially segregated. Black children went to all-black schools. White children went to all white schools.

The laws in southern states said that schools should be "separate but equal" for the races. In actuality, schools for blacks were usually not as good as those for whites.

In 1954, the United States Supreme Court had declared that segregation in public schools was unconstitutional. Separate schools, the Court reasoned, could not be equal. Black parents in several southern states tried to enroll their children in formerly all-white schools, but white southerners resisted.

In Little Rock, the Arkansas capital, blacks wanted to begin attending Little Rock Central High School. Governor Orville Faubus ordered the state's National Guard troops to keep blacks out of the school and to maintain order.

Dwight D. Eisenhower, then president of the United States, did not want a conflict with the southern states over segregation, but he could not tolerate Governor Faubus's open defiance of the federal government.

Commander in chief of all U.S. armed forces, President Eisenhower ordered the Army into Little Rock. U.S. soldiers were told to guard the students and make sure that no one harmed them. Many angry protests followed from hostile white citizens, but the black children went to the formerly all-white school.

Although over a hundred years separate the South Carolina and the Arkansas protests, the basic issue is very much the same. How much authority does the federal government have? How much authority do state governments have? When federal and state governments disagree, whose authority is superior? Can states resist federal authority?

These questions form the basis for this book. In it, you will read about one of the issues involved in the creation of the United States Constitution and the development of the United States system of government—the issue of states' rights.

Chapter 2

The Revolutionary Era

Members of the Continental Congress had been arguing for hours. Should the colonies declare their independence from Great Britain? Finally, on July 2, 1776, they voted. The resolution they adopted favored independence. Richard Henry Lee had written it. It said:

> Resolved, that these United Colonies are, and of right ought to be, free and independent States. . . .

Two days later, Congress adopted the Declaration of Independence, which was mostly written by Thomas Jefferson. Americans were breaking away from their mother country! The next year, Congress agreed upon the Articles of Confederation which provided for a confederacy to be known as the United States of America.

Even in these early days, people were concerned about the power the states would have as opposed to the power of the national government. Great Britain, with its king and Parliament, which made laws, had a strong central government. Americans wanted to create a government that differed somewhat from the British government.

Revenue was needed for the Army that the Continental Congress had authorized in 1776, but the colonies, remembering the trouble with England over taxation, had not granted Congress the power to levy taxes.

Congress could only divide its heavy Revolutionary War debts among the colonies and ask them to pay. Payment of the bills, though, could not be imposed by force by any single authority. The debts were largely ignored.

During the Revolution only the states had the right to impose and collect taxes. This was one example of states' rights.

The British government had the authority to draft men into the Army. "To draft" means to force to serve. Sometimes the British Navy kidnapped men and made them work on ships. Americans, therefore, saw the draft as another example of a government that was too strong.

The American government did not have the power to draft men into the Army. The states did. America used volunteers, and Congress asked each state to supply a certain number of soldiers. Some served as soldiers in the Continental Army, commanded by George Washington. Often, the soldiers from a state would be kept together in a fighting unit commanded by an officer from their own state.

Control over raising the Army was another example of states' rights during the Revolution. Limiting the power of the government was the idea behind these states' rights. Yet, in spite of the weakness of the national government, the nation, even before the states had adopted the Articles, won the Revolution.

In 1781, the states adopted the Articles of Confederation. They were America's first plan of government. They created a weak national government. Laws were passed in the legislature, called Congress, where each state had one vote. For an important

In 1775 George Washington became commander in chief of the Continental army.

measure such as taxation to become law every state had to vote in favor of it. This protected states' rights. Any state could block many national laws.

After the Revolution, Americans continued to be governed under the Articles of Confederation. In peacetime, the role of the states and the national government became clearer.

Under the Articles, the states carried the responsibility for most internal affairs. Internal affairs are events inside the country. The national government bore responsibility for external affairs, that is, relations with foreign countries.

The states, for example, controlled qualifications for voting and for holding office. States generally allowed only men to vote, in most cases only men who owned property. States often required men who held office to own a large amount of property.

The states controlled fund raising, too. This was very similar to the Revolutionary period. Congress could not levy or collect a tax. It could only set a certain amount it wanted the states to contribute. Some states attempted to meet the requests of Congress but the majority of states did not. Congress could do nothing about that.

Regulating trade was another states' right under the Articles of Confederation. Each state set its own tariff rate. Some states put taxes on products shipped from other states. The states even had the power to print their own money.

So, deciding who could vote and hold office, controlling fund raising, and regulating trade were states' rights under the Articles of Confederation. What then were the powers of the national government?

The national government could make treaties with foreign countries. Treaties are arrangements made by negotiation between governments. Unfortunately, most European countries did not want to make treaties with the United States government. They thought the United States was weak and poor and of no concern to them.

One thing the national government did do was to establish a post office. Government agents carried the mail.

Overall, the national government was weak. Americans wanted it that way. But the government under the Articles of Confederation turned out to be too weak.

The national government still could not draft soldiers. The nation depended on state militias. In 1786 the federal government asked the states to send groups of militiamen to Massachusetts. There, poor farmers were preventing the state supreme court from conducting business.

Daniel Shays and many of his followers had fought in the Revolution. But they had never been paid for their service. The national government was broke. It did not have enough money to pay its soldiers. The soldiers, on the other hand, could not pay their debts. Many of them had lost their homes or farms. Fortunately, enough volunteers showed up to prevent the seizure of an arsenal in Springfield in 1787 and make the farmers back down.

Many people thought that Shays' Rebellion was a close call. They believed the rebellion was proof of need for a stronger federal government.

Slavery was never to be allowed in the Northwest Territory, or in parts of it that became states, even if inhabitants wanted it.

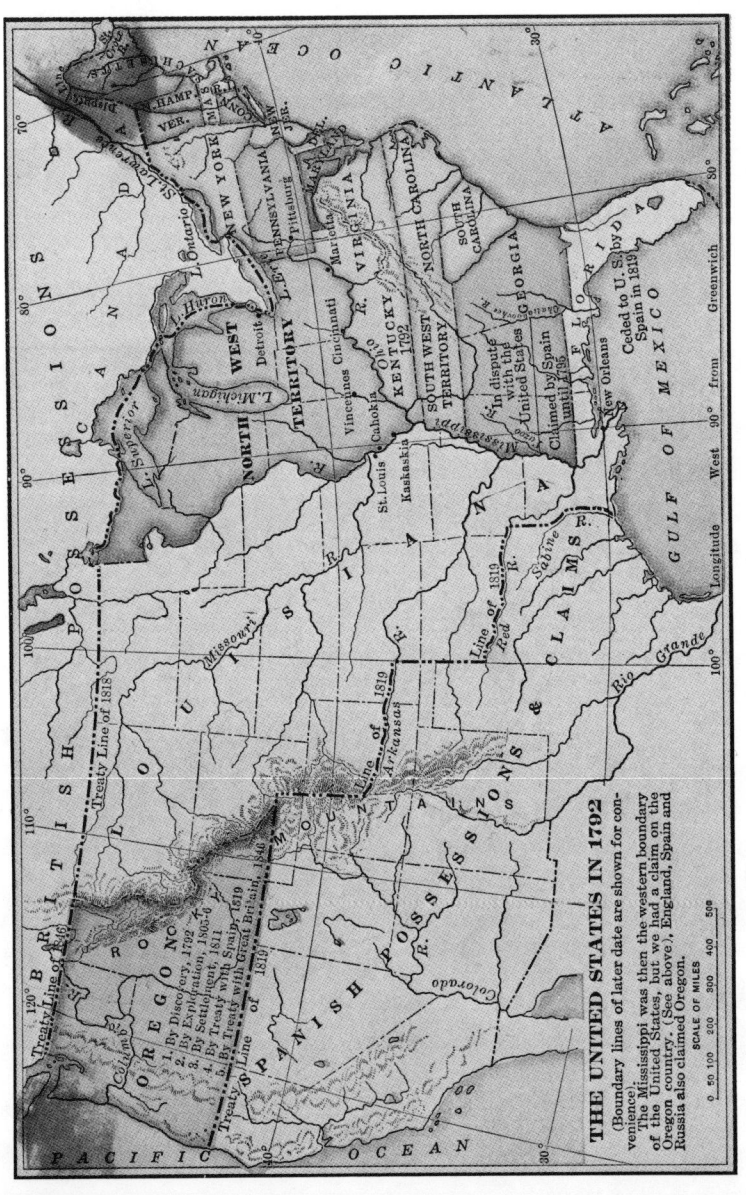

Even though the national government was weak, it was, however, successful in some areas. The government's success or failure depended on whether or not the states would agree among themselves.

Many of the states were concerned about territory that belonged to the nation, but was not yet part of any state. A big section of land was called the Northwest Territory. It lay to the west of the northern states. People who lived in the Northwest Territory were spread out over a lot of land.

In 1787 Congress passed a law known as the Northwest Ordinance. The Northwest Ordinance outlined the conditions under which parts of the Northwest Territory could be divided into states. When the population in an area grew to 60,000, it could be admitted into the Union as a state.

The Northwest Ordinance, however, removed one right that many people thought should be a states' right. That was the right to allow slavery. The Northwest Ordinance forbade slavery; it was never to be allowed in the Northwest Territory or in states that came out of it.

Many people, especially southerners, did not like that. They believed that people should be able to own slaves anywhere they wished.

But the Northwest Ordinance was evidence that, even under the Articles of Confederation, states' rights could sometimes be limited.

Chapter 3

The Constitution

The year was 1787. Important officials from all over the United States had been called to a meeting in Philadelphia.

The subject was the Articles of Confederation. Were they too weak? Or were wealthy people trying to start another government that was too powerful? Would the rights of the people be protected? What about the rights of the states—would they be lost?

This was the Constitutional Convention. Leaders all over the nation feared that a crisis was at hand. The Articles of Confederation were just not working, they thought. The plan of government needed changing.

Delegates to the Constitutional Convention were chosen by the state legislatures. Members of the state legislatures, you might remember, usually had to be property owners. The delegates, therefore, were generally well off financially. Most were lawyers. Many had helped write their states' constitutions.

Most of the delegates favored a stronger national government. One of the strongest supporters of states' rights, Patrick Henry of Virginia, a hero of the Revolution, had been chosen as a delegate,

In 1787 George Washington presided over the Constitutional Convention.

but he refused to serve. A lot of the leaders of the Revolution were not delegates to the Constitutional Convention.

But the most important leader in the Revolution, George Washington, was there. People admired Washington tremendously. His presence enhanced the importance of the meeting. Benjamin Franklin, who was now eighty-one years old, was there, too, as were James Madison and Alexander Hamilton. Madison would eventually become known as the Father of the Constitution. Hamilton, an influential New Yorker, favored a much stronger government.

The delegates were supposed to be rewriting the Articles of Confederation. But soon after discussions began, they decided to throw out the Articles altogether and write a new plan of government.

Large states wanted representation in Congress to be based on population. This would give them more power in making the laws. Delegates from Virginia suggested this plan. Virginia had one of the largest populations then.

New Jersey, a state with a small population, wanted representation by state. Each state should have the same number of votes in Congress, delegates from smaller states thought. This would protect their states' rights. This was the way representation had been arranged under the Articles of Confederation.

Delegates argued long and hard. Finally, they reached a compromise. A compromise is when each side gives up something in order to gain something else. Delegates decided to set up two houses in Congress. In order to become a law, a proposal would have to be passed by both houses.

Representation in one house would be based on population. That house was called the House of Representatives. Representation in the other house would be equal for each state. That was called the Senate. This compromise has been called the Great Compromise and it worked out the most serious disagreement among the delegates.

In the Great Compromise, the states gave up some of their power. Large states could outvote small states in the House of Representatives. Small states, however, had equal standing with large states in the Senate.

Several other disagreements arose. Some of the southern states wanted to continue the slave trade. The northern states and even some of the other southern states wanted to end the slave trade. Another compromise stated that the slave trade would not be restricted for twenty years. (After twenty years Congress outlawed the importation of slaves.)

Taxes formed the basis for another conflict. Should the national government be allowed to tax the people directly? What role would the states play? Congress was given the "power to lay and collect taxes." Furthermore, "all bills raising revenue shall originate in the House of Representatives." The delegates agreed that this was right because the House more truly represented all the people than the Senate did.

What about tariffs and exported goods? The southern states were especially concerned about these topics. Southerners carried on a great deal of trade with European countries. At that time, tobacco was the chief product, and later, cotton would become increasingly important.

Congress was given the power to impose tariffs, but with the condition that exports should not be subject to duties. States did not have the right to impose tariffs on exports and imports either between the states or to and from other countries.

Slaves were herded like cattle to southern slave markets.

The Constitutional Convention agreed that all treaties would require the approval of a two-thirds majority of the Senate. In the Senate, small states had just as much power as large ones. Southern states, therefore, stood on equal ground with northern states.

A number of other disagreements arose. After much arguing and discussing and compromising, the delegates had a plan they thought would work. But the Constitution had to be approved by two-thirds of the states in their own Constitutional Conventions.

Some of the strongest arguments against the new Constitution centered on worries about states' rights. To many people, the Constitution took away too many of the states' powers, as well as reduced the rights of individuals.

Under the Articles of Confederation, the national government had been a confederation. In a confederation, the central government is weak, and the individual units, the states, are strong. The Constitution created a federal government. In a federal government, the central, or national, government would be stronger.

People debated whether or not the Constitution should be ratified. "Ratifying" means voting that a measure should be approved. The people elected state conventions, which voted on the Constitution.

Nine state conventions ratified the Constitution within a year. This gave the required two-thirds majority. But what would happen in the other four states?

In Virginia, the argument continued. Patrick Henry was one of the leaders against the Constitution. George Washington and James Madison publicly supported it. During the debates, those who favored the Constitution promised to work for a bill of rights.

A bill of rights is a document designed to protect freedoms. It specifically safeguards individual rights. The other states that were holding out liked that idea, too. North Carolina especially supported a bill of rights. Promised a bill of rights and realizing they could not exist as separate countries, Virginia and New York ratified soon after New Hampshire, the ninth state. North Carolina and Rhode Island ratified later.

The first Congress that met under the Constitution developed the Bill of Rights. These rights are listed in the first ten amendments to the Constitution. An amendment is something that has been added to an original document.

Most of the Bill of Rights dealt with individual liberties. Freedom of religion, speech, peaceful assembly, and the press were guaranteed. The last two amendments formed a final restraint upon the national government.

The Ninth Amendment stated that listing certain rights in the Constitution did not mean that other rights had been taken away from the people. The Tenth Amendment reserved for the states those powers not specifically denied to them or assigned to the federal government.

The Constitution, therefore, set up a stronger central government than the United States had under the Articles of Confederation. Under the articles, any state could block most actions of the national government. Under the Constitution, the federal government could act even if some states opposed it.

But the federal government could act only in matters that the Constitution authorized. Specific powers and procedures were established that the government and its officials had to follow. Even the president had to obey the law.

Everything not "delegated" to the federal government was reserved for the states. "Everything" covers a lot of things, though. What role would the states actually play in the new government?

The problem of states' rights has been worked out in practice over a period of many years. Disagreements still occur. As situations developed involving states' rights, procedures set up in the Constitution have been followed. These procedures gradually did what they were designed to do. They let the new government adapt to new situations.

Chapter

4

The Age of Jefferson

The states ratified the Constitution. But agreement to adopt the Constitution did not mean that everyone would agree about how to make the new government work.

As you have seen, during the debate over the Constitution, those people who favored stronger government had supported the Constitution. They were called Federalists. Those who wanted to keep a weak central government usually opposed the Constitution. They were called Anti-Federalists.

The Constitution did not mention political parties. But people who held similar opinions tended to band together. Gradually, the Federalists and the Anti-Federalists became political parties.

President George Washington strongly supported the Constitution. His vice-president, John Adams, was later elected the second president. Adams and his political friends were known as the Federalist Party.

Thomas Jefferson was elected vice-president when Adams was elected president. But Jefferson and Adams disagreed on a number of issues. Jefferson and his followers were Anti-Federalists.

The Federalists did not want people to speak out against them and their ideas. Federalists in Congress passed a set of laws called the Alien and Sedition Acts. Aliens are residents who are not citizens of the United States. Sedition is conduct consisting of speaking, writing, or acting in such a way as to cause rebellion against an established government.

Most of the people who had just moved to the United States were poor. They generally favored weaker government and lower taxes. As soon as they were eligible to become citizens and vote, they usually voted Republican (Anti-Federalists were later called Republicans).

During the early years of the Constitution, people could become citizens after they had lived in the United States for five years. One of the Alien Acts ruled that they had to wait fourteen years. This cut down on future Republican votes.

Under the Sedition Act people could be fined and put in jail for criticizing the government or government officials. This seriously hurt freedom of speech and freedom of the press. Several Republican newspaper editors were thrown into jail.

Jefferson and the Republicans, of course, deplored the Alien and Sedition Acts. Jefferson had written most of the Declaration of Independence. He was a champion of free speech and free newspapers.

Thomas Jefferson and James Madison wrote a set of resolutions. Jefferson secretly sent his to friends in Kentucky. The Kentucky legislature passed them in November 1798 and November 1799, calling them the Kentucky Resolutions. Madison's ideas were adopted by the Virginia legislature in December 1798. These were called the Virginia Resolutions.

The Kentucky and Virginia Resolutions set forth certain ideas about states' rights. They said that the federal government had been created by an agreement of the states. Therefore, the state—even one state—should be able to decide whether the national government was overstepping its authority.

Jefferson and Madison believed that the federal government did not have the power to enact and enforce the Alien and Sedition Acts. No federal law should be able to take away freedom of speech and freedom of the press.

The legislatures of Kentucky and Virginia agreed. Kentucky and Virginia felt they should not have to obey laws they disagreed with. In other words, Virginia and Kentucky should be able to nullify the Alien and Sedition Acts.

No other state, however, went along with Kentucky and Virginia on this matter. Many people argued that the states did not create the federal government; the people did. States, therefore, could not nullify federal laws. Nullification, these people said, was not a states' right.

If states could not nullify a federal law, then who could? That question was answered in 1803.

Thomas Jefferson had been elected the third president by that time. James Madison was his secretary of state. The outgoing president, John Adams, had appointed a justice of the peace just before he left office.

But Secretary Madison would not let the appointee, William Marbury, take office, so Marbury sued Madison. The case was appealed all the way to the Supreme Court. The Court ruled that the action Madison had taken in blocking Marbury from his job was unconstitutional. That means the government had done something that the court believed to be in conflict with the Constitution.

The case of *Marbury* v. *Madison*, therefore, established the power of judicial review. Judicial review is the process whereby the Court decides whether a law is constitutional. A law or an act that the Supreme Court decides is unconstitutional is nullified. States do not have the right of nullification.

Foreign affairs were considered part of the national government's role even under the Articles of Confederation. In the early 1800s, though, a situation arose in which some states tried to extend states' rights even to foreign affairs.

Britain and France had been enemies for a long time. Each wanted to control large parts of the world and to dominate world trade. In the early 1800s, they went to war.

Each country tried to shut off the other country's trade with foreign nations. But Americans believed they should be able to trade with anyone they wished. The United States wanted to be neutral. "Neutral" means not taking sides.

In addition to trying to control American trade, the British were doing something else that made Americans extremely angry. British warships would stop American ships and take off sailors. The British would make these sailors work on British ships.

Some of the sailors were deserters, men who had been in the British Navy and later ran away. The British thought they had a right to take these sailors back; Americans disagreed. But even worse, sometimes the British took American sailors who had never been in the British Navy.

In 1807, President Jefferson responded by persuading Congress to pass the Embargo Act. An embargo is a refusal to trade. American ships were not allowed to leave port. Jefferson knew that if American ships did not sail the seas, then the British could not attack them. Keeping the ships at home, he hoped, would keep the United States out of the European war.

But people in the New England states hated the embargo.

They made their living by shipping. The embargo cut off their incomes. Some New England states talked about seceding. Seceding is withdrawing from the Union, or separating from the United States. Other New England states considered nullifying the embargo law.

This time, the federal government gave in. In 1809, the embargo law was changed. Trade with England and France was still prohibited, since they were at war, but Americans could trade with any other country.

The conflict with Great Britain continued, though. British ships kept on capturing American sailors. Many Americans believed the British were stirring up the Indians. And some Americans wanted the United States to capture Canada, which Great Britain still owned.

In 1812 the United States and Great Britain went to war. James Madison was president then. Once again, the New England states opposed the action of the federal government. Shippers in New England had been making lots of money. Trade was good, even though sailors were still being taken off ships.

Trade with Great Britain was still against the law. But shippers in New England traded with the British in Canada. People living in the New England states began to talk about making a treaty with Great Britain, even though the United States was at war with the British.

Late in 1814, representatives of the New England states met at Hartford, Connecticut. A number of the delegates to the Hartford Convention wanted their states to secede from the United States. Fortunately, a majority of the delegates voted against secession. New England stayed in the United States. But the ideas of nullification and secession would come up again in the future.

In the War of 1812 the American sloop of war Wasp *captured the English sloop* Forlic.

Meanwhile, the United States fought the British to a draw in the War of 1812. Once again, the supposedly more powerful British failed to beat the Americans.

The question of slavery as a states' right came up again in 1819.

As you read in Chapter 2, slavery was prohibited in the Northwest Territory. Under President Jefferson the United States had bought a huge section of land called the Louisiana Purchase. He bought this land from France in 1803. It joined the Northwest Territory.

People began moving into the Louisiana Territory. Some moved from southern states. They took slaves with them. The land in the Louisiana Territory was good for farming. The Indian problem had subsided somewhat. Americans had greater control over the territory. So movement into the area increased.

By 1818 enough people lived in one part of the Louisiana Territory to apply for statehood. This section was called Missouri. When Missouri applied to be a state, Congress said that no more slaves would be allowed there. And slaves already living in Missouri would have to be freed.

People in Missouri wanted to keep their slaves. Southern states were angry, too. They thought that this was a move by northern states to start ending slavery all over the country.

In the Senate at this time, there were eleven free states and eleven slave states. If Missouri came into the United States as a free state, then the free states could outvote the slave states. If Missouri came in as a slave state, then the slave states would have the advantage.

After much debate, representatives of the states compromised. In 1821 Missouri entered the United States as a slave state. But to keep the balance between slave and free states, a section of

Massachusetts was allowed to break away to become the free state of Maine.

In an effort to prevent further disagreement like this, Congress passed a law that no new state north of the southern border of Missouri could allow slavery. Congress had, for the time being, limited the right of future states to decide whether they would be free or slave.

Chapter 5

Civil War

Before 1850 each of the disagreements over states' rights had been settled by compromise. The states gained authority in some cases and lost authority in others. But around 1850, problems began to develop in which some states were less willing to compromise.

For quite some time, southern states had been claiming slavery as a states' right. No federal law should be able to outlaw slavery, they believed. But many northerners opposed slavery. People who wanted to end, or abolish, slavery were called abolitionists.

The United States fought a war with Mexico from 1846 to 1848 and won. As a part of the peace treaty, Mexico gave the United States a tremendous section of land. This land stretched from Texas to California, almost the entire Southwest.

At first, Americans celebrated the acquisition of all this land. But then abolitionists and others realized that much of this land was just right for growing cotton. And if people were growing cotton, they would want to have slaves.

After many people had moved into California, it applied to become a state. A large number of these people were miners who had come in 1849 looking for gold, and were called "Forty-niners." Californians did not grow much cotton and therefore did not need slaves. California asked to come into the Union as a free state.

By this time, there were fifteen slave and fifteen free states. The balance of slave to free states had been maintained. If California came into the Union as a free state, it would upset this balance.

Southerners were upset by another problem. Abolitionists had been trying to put an end to slavery in the District of Columbia, the nation's capital, for a long time. Southerners did not want slavery abolished anywhere.

In addition, southerners were angry over their inability to reclaim runaway slaves. Slaves who managed to escape went north. Sometimes abolitionists, free blacks, or other escaped slaves helped runaways escape. At that time, slaves who got as far as a free state became free.

Southerners wanted escaped slaves brought back to the South. Since they thought slavery was a states' right, they thought slaves were their property. And lost or stolen property should be returned to its owner, southerners claimed.

Congress worked out one last compromise, the Compromise of 1850. Henry Clay of Kentucky, known as the Great Compromiser for his work on the Compromise of 1820 and other agreements, now tried again to get the southern and northern states to compromise. Clay, who was seventy-three years old in 1850, received skillful support from Stephen A. Douglas of Illinois, a fiery speaker.

However, the speech that convinced northerners to support a compromise was made by Daniel Webster of New Hampshire. Webster was a dynamic speaker, known for his ability to persuade people. This time he persuaded northerners to make concessions to the South.

Representing Kentucky in the House and Senate for almost fifty years, Henry Clay influenced compromises that determined where slavery was to be allowed.

John C. Calhoun, now sixty-three years old, gathered his energies to speak for the South. But he was not well and so weak that someone else had to read his speech for him. Not long after the debate was over, Calhoun died. His last words were, "The South! The South! God knows what will become of her!"

The compromise that these men worked so hard to achieve gave something to both North and South. California was admitted to the United States in 1850 as a free state. Slave trade was outlawed in the District of Columbia. People could still own slaves in the capital, but they could not buy or sell them. These actions pleased the North.

Two parts of the Compromise of 1850 won favor in the South. In the land won from Mexico, new states would be able to vote on slavery. This meant of course that slavery might be allowed in new states. In addition, a new, strong fugitive slave law was passed. Runaway slaves, even if they reached the North, were to be returned to their owners.

To the South, the states' right to allow slavery had been maintained. But in one sense the Compromise of 1850 backfired. Many people in the northern states did not want to become involved in the capture and return of fugitive slaves. Some who up to this time had not been against slavery turned against it. They could hardly ignore slavery when slaves were being captured in their own towns.

Strong unpleasant feelings between the North and the South grew during the 1850s. Northerners became more and more opposed to slavery. Southerners resisted attacks on their way of life.

In 1854 Congress passed a law that made the situation worse. The House of Representatives was considering admitting two new states, Kansas and Nebraska. Southerners, along with some northern and western supporters, wanted Kansas and Nebraska to be able to vote on the issue of slavery.

But part of these lands were in the section ruled "forever free" by the Missouri Compromise of 1820. Allowing people there to vote on the issue of slavery would violate this compromise. But allowing people to vote on slavery would strengthen the cause of states' rights.

Senator Stephen A. Douglas strongly supported the Kansas-Nebraska Act. Douglas believed in letting peole vote on important issues. But he was also trying to get southern support. He wanted to be President.

The Kansas-Nebraska Act repealed the Missouri Compromise and allowed the two new territories to determine whether they would be free or slave. No one really expected Nebraska to vote for slavery. It lay to the west of a free state. But Kansas became a battleground over slavery. People who were for and against slavery actually fought and killed each other in a small war. The battle continued for several years. Eventually, Kansas entered the Union as a free state.

Meanwhile, a Supreme Court decision fanned the flames of anger. Dred Scott was a slave. He had been taken into Illinois, a free state, by his owner. Then they went back to Missouri, a slave state. After Scott's owner died, abolitionists sued to get freedom for Scott. His having been on free soil, they said, had made him a free man.

But the Supreme Court ruled that Dred Scott was not free. The Court said that slaves were property. Under the Constitution, property could not be taken away without proper legal arrangements. The Court said that freeing a slave amounted to taking away property.

Roger B. Taney, Chief Justice of the Supreme Court at that

Campaigning for a seat in the Senate, Abraham Lincoln and Stephen A. Douglas debated the slavery issue. Lincoln lost the election.

time, was a southerner from Maryland. Maryland was a slave state. Taney wrote that the Constitution did not include slaves as citizens. Therefore, slaves could not enter into lawsuits, because they were not citizens.

The Dred Scott decision strengthened states' rights tremendously. It meant that slavery could exist in any state.

At the same time that the Kansas-Nebraska Act and the Dred Scott decision were creating tensions, a new political party was growing, the Republican Party. (The Republican Party of Thomas Jefferson had died out. This was a new party.) The Republican Party was founded by people who believed that Congress should have the right to limit the growth of slavery.

The Republican view, of course, was considered anti–states' rights and antislavery. Southerners did not like Republicans and believed that they were generally abolitionists. Many Republicans were abolitionists, but many were not. They did not favor equal rights for black people or the abolition of slavery in the South. They simply wanted to stop the spread of slavery to new states. But southerners regarded even that as a violation of states' rights.

In 1858 the Republican Party in Illinois nominated Abraham Lincoln as their candidate for the United States Senate. At that time it was the state legislatures, not the people, who voted for U.S. senators. The Democratic nominee, seeking reelection, was Stephen A. Douglas.

Lincoln and Douglas met each other in a series of debates. The statements these candidates made put the issues of the times into focus.

Lincoln stated, "In my opinion . . . a house divided against itself cannot stand." By "house," he meant the United States. By "divided against itself," he meant some states should not allow slavery while others forbade it. This disagreement, he thought, would eventually create a crisis.

Douglas felt that slavery and freedom could exist peaceably in the same country. He said that people should be able to allow or prohibit slavery, as they wished, in new states. The government should not interfere with slavery in the South, Douglas said.

Douglas defeated Lincoln in the election in the Illinois legislature.

By 1860 the Republican Party had grown in strength. But its strength was almost all in the North. The Republicans nominated Abraham Lincoln for president in the election of 1860.

At the Democratic Party convention, southern states demanded a proslavery position. They wanted the party to declare that slavery could not be outlawed anywhere. Northern delegates wanted to allow new states to vote on slavery. Slavery in new states, therefore, could be allowed or prohibited, as the people wished.

Southern states walked out of the convention. They formed their own new party and nominated John C. Breckinridge as their candidate for president. The rest of the Democrats nominated Stephen A. Douglas. A fourth party, the Constitutional Unionists, nominated John Bell, a southerner. They wanted to hold the nation together any way they could.

Abraham Lincoln was elected president. Southern states, led by South Carolina, were furious. They believed that Lincoln was an abolitionist. Lincoln, they thought, would destroy the southern way of life.

Late in 1860, South Carolina seceded from the United States. This means that the state withdrew from the nation. Within a few months, several other southern states joined South Carolina. Even-

In South Carolina soldiers fired on Fort Sumter after it was reinforced by the Union.

tually, eleven states seceded, forming the Confederate States of America.

The United States had split up. This was the crisis that Abraham Lincoln had warned about. President Lincoln, however, believed that secession was not a states' right. A president, he believed, must preserve the Union. And in 1861, soldiers in South Carolina fired on a Union fort, Fort Sumter, in Charleston, South Carolina, when the Union tried to send in reinforcements. Southerners claimed that the reinforcement expedition was an invasion of a sovereign state.

War soon followed. Before the Civil War ended, more Americans would be killed than all those in all the other wars this nation has ever fought. Deciding this question of states' rights cost the nation a large toll in lives and in dollars.

In the South, the Confederate States set up a government that claimed to respect states' rights. The Confederate constitution stated that the southern government had been formed by the states. Tariffs were against the law. The Confederate president, Jefferson Davis, had a six-year term, but he could not be reelected. The right to own slaves was guaranteed.

As war drew on, it became clear that the Union was stronger than the Confederacy. The Union had more people, more soldiers, more money, more railroads, and more industry. The Union could make what it needed.

The Confederate States had hoped for help from foreign countries that bought southern cotton. But Great Britain and other European countries would not get heavily involved in an American war. Britain supplied some ships to the Confederacy, but that help was not enough. The Confederacy lost the war.

The most serious question of states' rights had been answered. States did not have the right to secede from the United States.

Chapter 6

Reconstruction

The period after the Civil War is known as Reconstruction. This is when the nation was being put back together, or reconstructed.

A series of constitutional amendments and federal laws were passed after the war. Slavery was outlawed, and blacks were given the right of citizenship.

Many southerners, however, did not want to give blacks equal rights. They fought back with a series of state laws of their own. These state laws held back the growth of equal rights.

As the Civil War drew to a close, President Lincoln and Congress began to debate how the South should be readmitted to the Union. Lincoln offered to readmit any southern state in which 10 percent of the number of the state's voters in 1860 would swear to support the United States and abide by the Constitution.

As a part of this plan, Lincoln promised that the states would be allowed to decide how to deal with slavery. The federal government would not interfere. This would have turned the regulation of civil rights into a states' right.

These measures reflected President Lincoln's belief that the

United States (that is, the northern states) fought the Civil War mainly to preserve the Union. He wanted to make it as easy as possible for the southern states to rejoin the Union.

Lincoln was reelected president in 1864. Part of the Republican Party's platform had called for an end to slavery. In 1865 Congress passed the Thirteenth Amendment to the United States Constitution. The Thirteenth Amendment outlawed slavery.

A constitutional amendment must be ratified by three-fourths of the states before it becomes part of the Constitution, though. So the Amendment was sent to the state legislatures for ratification. By the end of the year, twenty-seven states ratified the Thirteenth Amendment, all that were needed.

The Thirteenth Amendment is significant in the history of states' rights for two reasons. It eliminated slavery as a states' right, while, at the same time, it illustrated the states' right to accept or reject amendments to the Constitution. Since the states must approve a proposed amendment, they have the power to accept or reject any amendment that gives them rights or takes them away.

Opposition to President Lincoln's plan for Reconstruction developed in Congress. A number of Congressmen believed the president was being too easy on the South. They wanted the South to be punished.

Before Lincoln could carry his plan further, he was murdered, shot by a man named John Wilkes Booth. Vice-President Andrew Johnson, who became president at Lincoln's death, was not popular with Congress. He tried to continue much of Lincoln's plan for the South. But members of Congress were suspicious of him because he was from Tennessee, a southern state. And he was promoting a plan that they thought was easy on the South.

Meanwhile, the southern states began to pass laws regarding the way blacks were to be treated. Blacks could not vote or hold office, own weapons, quit their jobs, or be members of juries. In some states, a black man who did not have a job could be arrested. If convicted of vagrancy, or loafing around, the man would be made to work on road construction gangs. This was much like slavery.

Congress passed a law called the Civil Rights Act, which outlawed these so-called Black Codes. But President Johnson vetoed, or rejected, the Civil Rights Act. Congress can override a presidential veto, or pass the law anyway, by a two-thirds vote. And Congress did just that. In 1866 a group of anti-South, pro-Civil Rights Republicans, called Radical Republicans, gathered enough support to pass the Civil Rights Act.

The Civil Rights Act declared that all persons born in the United States were citizens and should have equal rights. The Civil Rights Act, therefore, took away what the South believed was a states' right. Southern states no longer had the right to treat blacks differently from whites.

But many people argued that the Civil Rights Act was unconstitutional. Members of Congress, therefore, decided to make the ideas in the Civil Rights Act a part of the Constitution. If these ideas were added to the Constitution itself, then they could not be declared unconstitutional.

In 1866, Congress passed the Fourteenth Amendment to the Constitution. Like the Civil Rights Act, the Fourteenth Amendment declared that everyone born in the United States, including blacks, was a citizen, and that no state could take away a citizen's life, liberty, or property without "due process of law."

Setting up conditions for voting was another states' right. States were allowed to set up requirements for voting, such as age or the ability to read and write.

The Fourteenth Amendment ruled that if a state denied any

President Andrew Johnson's impeachment ended with a verdict of not guilty.

of its "male inhabitants" the right to vote, the state would proportionally lose some of its members in Congress. Northern states could deny their few black residents the right to vote and lose little or no representation in Congress. It was the Southern states, with their large black population, that would suffer if they denied blacks the right to vote.

After Congress passed the Fourteenth Amendment, it was sent to the states for ratification. But the southern states refused to ratify it. The three-fourths majority needed to make it a constitutional amendment could not be raised.

But Congress would not give up. Members passed the Reconstruction Act. This Act threw out southern state governments. Federal troops were sent to run the South.

Southern states were required to call constitutional conventions, at which states, as the price of readmission into the Union, had to adopt the Fourteenth Amendment.

By 1868 most of the southern states had complied with the Reconstruction Acts and had become part of the United States again. Meanwhile, President Johnson's opponents in the House of Representatives had voted to impeach the president. "To impeach" means to bring to trial on the basis of an accusation. They felt that, like Lincoln, he was too lenient with the South and they wanted to get rid of him. When the Senate tried the president, they found him not guilty—but by only one vote.

Radical Republicans, however, had established their strength. New federal laws were passed that took away a number of rights that had belonged to the states. Among these was the power to try certain types of cases in court.

Before the Reconstruction Acts, state courts had dealt with most crimes of violence. But in the 1870s, Congress gave that authority to federal courts in certain cases. If violence or threats were used to keep people from voting, then federal courts took the case.

Federal courts, therefore, would try any cases that involved former slaves who had been threatened or attacked. Very few people, however, were brought to trial under these laws.

The strength of southern state governments had been reduced or curtailed. In 1868, Ulysses S. Grant, supported by the Radicals, was nominated by the Republican Party, which went so far as to acclaim the "success" of Reconstruction. Grant was elected and in 1872 he was reelected.

In the presidential election of 1876, none of the candidates won a majority in the electoral college. The electoral college is the group that officially elects a president. When no candidate wins an election, the election must, according to the Constitution, be decided by the House of Representatives.

The Republicans claimed that many votes in southern states had been illegal, especially in Florida, Louisiana, and South Carolina. Congress created an electoral commission of eight Republicans and seven Democrats to investigate. The contested votes were awarded to Republican candidate Rutherford B. Hayes. Southern Democrats agreed to accept the verdict in return for the withdrawal of all remaining federal troops from South Carolina and Louisiana, ending Reconstruction. The southern states thus regained control of their own affairs.

Chapter 7

States' Rights Through the 1930s

After Reconstruction, government by conservative whites returned to the South. Challenges to civil rights, individual rights guaranteed by the Bill of Rights, began immediately. Gradually, the rights that had been won by blacks after the Civil War were reduced. States began to reassert their authority in the area of civil rights.

The first major legal challenge to civil rights in the South came before Reconstruction was over. Louisiana had passed a law in 1869 that gave one company the right to butcher almost all the animals being processed for food in New Orleans.

Other companies sued. They claimed that their not being allowed to share in the animal slaughtering business in New Orleans was illegal. They claimed such a law took away their business. A business, they argued, is property. Therefore the Louisiana law was unconstitutional because it took away property without due process of law.

The Fourteenth Amendment did say that the property of a citizen could not be taken away without due process of law. But the United States Supreme Court ruled that there was a difference between citizens of the United States and citizens of an individual state.

The right to due process, the Court stated, was subject to state regulation. So were other civil rights. These rights were considered state-controlled rights. The protection of civil rights, therefore, was up to the states.

Other civil rights came under attack in the 1880s. The Civil Rights Acts passed during Reconstruction said it was illegal to treat black people unfairly in hotels, theaters, and public transportation. Treating people unfairly because of their race is called discrimination.

The Supreme Court ruled that establishing different rules for whites and blacks was legal. Black people had been freed from slavery, but they had not been guaranteed equal treatment. Discrimination, therefore, was legal.

Supreme Court Justice John Marshall Harlan disagreed with the Court's decision. When a Supreme Court justice, or judge, disagrees, he may write a dissenting opinion. "To dissent" means to disagree.

Justice Harlan's dissent said that laws discriminating on the basis of race should be illegal. Civil rights, Harlan believed, should be the same in all states. States should not have the power to regulate civil rights.

But the decision of the Supreme Court's majority was law. Racial discrimination was legal. And southern states had passed numerous laws that restricted the rights of blacks.

These laws were similar to the Black Codes. They required strict separation of the races. Black children were required to go to separate schools. Blacks could not eat in white restaurants. Blacks could not buy property in white sections of town.

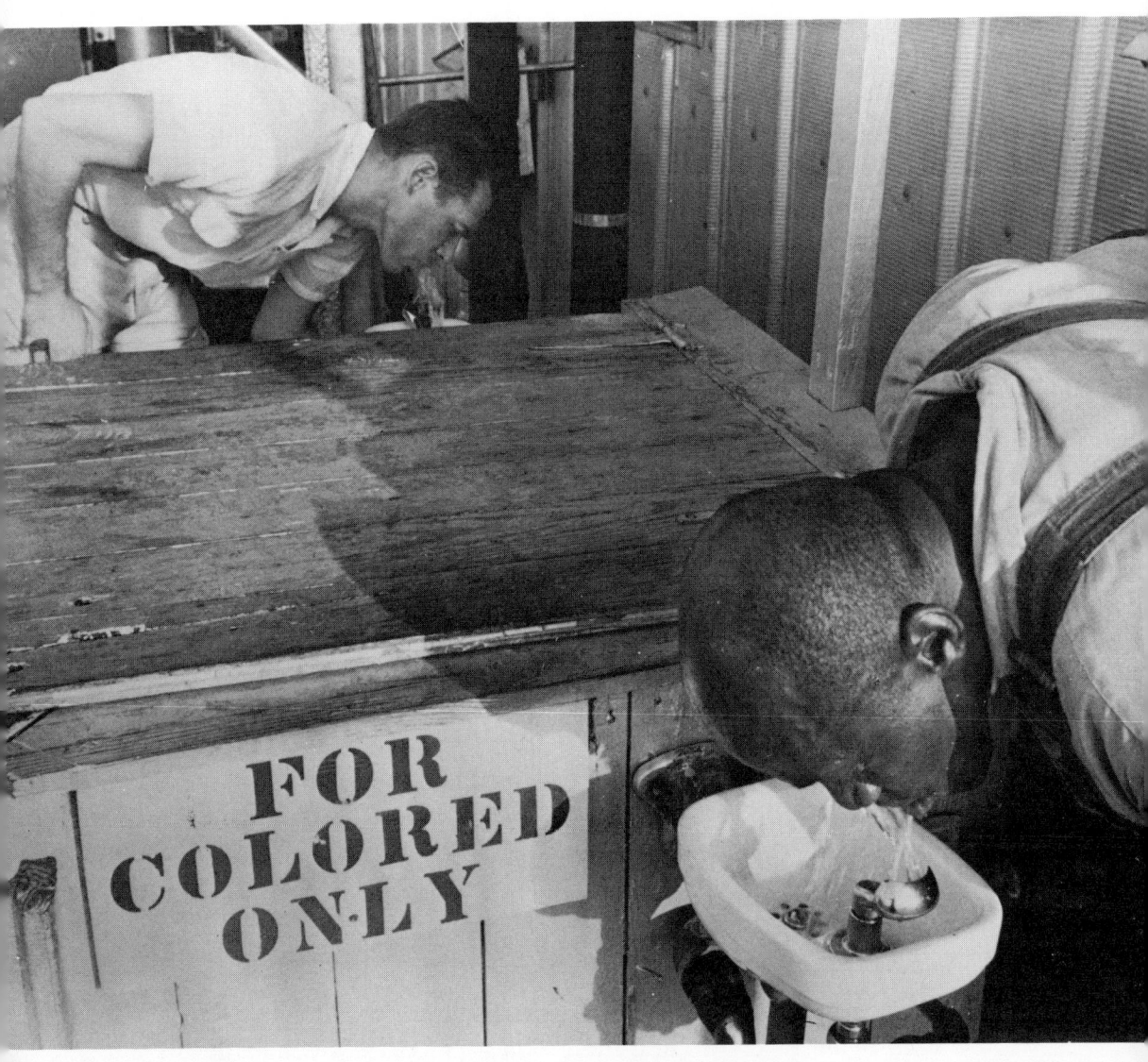

Until recently many areas and facilities in the South were segregated.

These restrictions were approved by the Supreme Court. A man named Homer Plessy filed suit in Louisiana in 1896. Plessy had been arrested when he tried to sit in a railroad car that was for "whites only." The law in Louisiana said that whites and blacks had to sit in separate railroad cars.

The Supreme Court decided that such arrangements were legal. States could require separate facilities for black and white people. This idea was called "separate but equal." Supposedly, the arrangements made for whites and blacks would be equal. In practice, however, this was hardly ever the case.

Once again, Justice Harlan dissented. He said that the Constitution did not recognize a "ruling class." No race should hold power over another, Harlan claimed.

"Separate but equal," however, became the law of the land. Regulating civil rights was considered a states' right, at least for a period of time. Laws discriminating against blacks remained in effect.

In other areas, however, states' rights began to decline. Railroads provided a great service to the people of the United States. Goods could be transported farther and faster than ever before, and in greater quantity.

But railroad companies often did things that some people thought were unfair. Railroads would give lower prices to larger customers. They would negotiate rates. Smaller customers, especially farmers, who needed to ship goods by rail were paying higher fees for the service.

At first, states were in charge of railroad regulation. "Regulation" means controlling the business practices of companies in order to protect the public. But state regulation was not very effective. Because the railroads carried goods from one state into another, no one state could regulate the railroad companies. In addition, the Supreme Court ruled in 1886 that states could not set rates for railroads.

In 1887, therefore, Congress passed the Interstate Commerce Act. The Act was a federal law that gave the power of regulating railroads to the federal government. The Act outlawed, among other things, charging higher rates per mile for short distances than for long distances. Railroads could not get together and set prices anymore.

The Interstate Commerce Act was not very strong, though. Railroad companies were often able to charge whatever price they wanted.

Over the years, Congress made the Interstate Commerce Act stronger. A federal commission could regulate railroad rates. The practice of giving some customers part of their freight rates back was made illegal.

The Interstate Commerce Act made a states' rights principle clearer. States can regulate trade inside the state. But the federal government has the power to regulate interstate trade, or trade that takes place between states.

Several new constitutional amendments took away other rights that had once belonged to the states.

The power to tax had been a source of disagreement for a long time. In 1913 the states ratified the Sixteenth Amendment to the Constitution. The Sixteenth Amendment authorized a federal income tax.

The Amendment also said that the taxes collected did not have to be divided among the states in any way. The federal government was free to use the money as it saw fit. The Sixteenth Amendment, therefore, created a direct tax for the federal government. The states had no control over the funds.

The Seventeenth Amendment was adopted in 1913 as well. Before that time, United States senators had been appointed by state legislatures. The appointment of senators was a states' right. But the Seventeenth Amendment gave the people the right to elect senators. Direct election of senators took away another states' right.

The Nineteenth Amendment to the Constitution was ratified in 1920. States had the right to establish requirements for voting, but the Nineteenth Amendment said that the right to vote could no longer be denied on account of sex. States could still set voting requirements, but being male could not be one of them.

States also had the power to regulate the manufacture and sale of alcoholic beverages. Some states allowed liquor to be sold by the drink. Others allowed alcohol to be sold only in bottles, which had to be drunk at home or in private. In some places, alcohol was illegal altogether.

In 1919, the Eighteenth Amendment took away the states' right to control alcohol. The Amendment said that alcoholic beverages could not be manufactured or sold anywhere in the United States. But the outlawing, or prohibition, of alcoholic beverages proved impossible to enforce. People manufactured liquor illegally, and lots of people bought it. Respect for the law began to decline.

In 1933, the Twenty-first Amendment repealed the Eighteenth Amendment. "Repeal" means to take back or put an end to. The Twenty-first Amendment made the regulation of alcoholic beverages a states' right again.

One other development contributed to the reduction of states' rights in the 1930s. The worst depression in the history of the United States struck the economy. A depression is an overall decline in economic activity.

In 1916 women marched for the vote—
they got it in 1920 (Amendment XIX).

President Franklin D. Roosevelt's New Deal was not without its critics.

Millions of people lost their jobs. Banks took back homes and farms when people could not make their mortgage payments. The banks could not resell the homes and farms because too many other people were out of work. Then the banks went broke. Businesses all over the country failed.

With the economy in such terrible condition, people looked to the federal government for help. The states did not have enough money to fix the economy. The depression was too widespread. The economy could not be repaired state by state. The nation as a whole had to pull together.

President Franklin D. Roosevelt asked Congress to create special federal programs to pull the country out of the depression. These programs gave people jobs and helped banks and businesses to recover. By the 1940s, the depression had weakened.

President Roosevelt's programs, called the New Deal, did not attack states' rights directly. But the effect was to direct people's attention toward the federal government. In the long run this resulted in a reduction in the role of the states in American government.

Chapter 8

States' Rights from the 1930s to Today

From the 1930s until the present, a number of attempts were made to strengthen states' rights. Most of these efforts grew out of the civil rights issue. But the overall trend was to cut down on the influence of states' rights, at least until very recently. During the 1930s and the 1940s, the Supreme Court reached a number of decisions affecting states' rights. Generally, these decisions shifted more power to the federal government and away from the states. Areas that had once been considered parts of states' rights came under the influence of the federal government.

Federal laws were upheld that placed more people under federally sponsored retirement, the Social Security Act. The federal government assumed more responsibility for regulating working and safety conditions. Housing programs were established.

The power of the federal government to regulate buying and selling of stocks, or shares of ownership, in private companies was upheld. Federal farm programs were ruled legal.

The most significant changes, though, came in the area of civil rights. In the late 1940s, President Harry S. Truman spoke

President Harry Truman expressed determination to use the power of the federal government to guarantee equal opportunity for all Americans.

out against lynching. Lynching was the practice of hanging a person accused of a crime without holding a trial first. Usually, it was a black who was lynched.

In 1947 a committee appointed by President Truman issued a report concerning civil rights in America. The report told Americans that discrimination and segregation, or separation by race, should be eliminated from laws in the United States.

As you recall from above, the enforcement of civil rights had been mostly left up to the states. Truman, however, stepped in and asked Congress to pass a civil rights law. Congress refused.

So the president took direct action in some areas. Truman ordered that a company doing business with the federal government could not discriminate on the basis of race. If it did, the government's business with the company would cease.

Truman was a Democrat. In the presidential election of 1948, a group of southerners within his own party broke away and started a new political party, called the States' Rights Party. This party stood for state regulation of civil rights because it opposed civil rights for blacks.

The effort gained little support nationwide, and President Truman won the election, even without support from the States' Rights Party.

Education was another field that had been largely left to the states. But by the 1950s, the federal government was providing considerable aid to education. The government realized that the nation must have educated citizens. Democracy requires people who can make political decisions. National defense depends on education, too.

Education was at the heart of one of the most important Supreme Court decisions of the age. In 1954, the Supreme Court declared racial segregation in public schools unconstitutional.

Many southerners were upset. Their schools had been racially segregated since the 1860s. Some southern states passed laws that were similar to the nullification acts of the pre–Civil War years. These laws were based on the idea that states had the right to decide which federal laws and which Supreme Court decision they would obey.

But the times were changing. In 1955, Rosa Parks, a black, refused to give her seat to a white man on a bus in Alabama. A federal court soon declared the state's bus segregation ordinance unconstitutional. In 1957 federal troops were sent to Arkansas to escort black students into a previously all-white shool. In 1960, four black college students began a wave of sit-ins when they refused to move from a Woolworth lunch counter where they were denied service. In 1970, a district court judge ordered extensive busing of elementary school children in North Carolina, carrying blacks to whites' schools and whites to blacks' schools to achieve a balance. Adjustment to desegregation has taken several decades and can still hardly be called an American way of life.

Another civil rights issue involved voting rights. As you read above, the states have the right to set requirements for voting. In many states, especially in the south, people were required to pay a tax in order to vote. This was called a poll tax. In 1962 President John F. Kennedy asked Congress to pass, and the people to support, a constitutional amendment outlawing poll taxes. The Twenty-fourth Amendment did that. In 1963, he asked Congress to pass a Civil Rights Act. But before the bill, or proposed act, could be considered, President Kennedy was murdered. On November 23, 1963, he was shot while riding in a parade in Dallas, Texas, and Vice-President Lyndon B. Johnson became president.

President Johnson urged Congress to act on the Civil Rights bill. In 1964, the bill was passed. The Civil Rights Act of 1964 outlawed racial discrimination in voting, jobs, public accommodations, and so forth. Moreover, it authorized the federal government to act directly against people accused of violating the law. The states were not responsible for enforcing the Act.

A Supreme Court decision in 1964, in a case known as *Baker v. Carr*, cut down on another states' right. This, too, was related to civil rights.

States had the right to draw districts for representation in Congress. But some districts contained many more people than others. This weakened the representation of some people. The Court decision ordered states to redraw congressional districts so that they contained about the same number of people.

In 1968, Richard Nixon ran on the Republican ticket for president. He campaigned against this growing power of the federal government, saying that more power should be reserved for the states. Nixon was elected.

Presidents can ask Congress to pass new laws. For some time Congress had been considering sharing federal tax money, or revenue, with the states. President Nixon convinced Congress to pass the Revenue Sharing Act. The Act required the federal government each year to return to the states a portion of the taxes it collected. This tended to strengthen state finances. It also gave the states increased status in relation to the federal government.

In addition, President Nixon was careful to nominate to the Supreme Court justices who were conservative. He hoped they would make decisions that would stem the growth of the powers of the federal government.

Other presidents have appointed justices who agreed with their views, but Nixon had more opportunities than most presidents. While Nixon was president, four justices died or retired, and to fill the vacancies he was able to appoint four conservative justices.

A few Supreme Court decisions influenced by justices that Nixon appointed have strengthened states' rights. In 1976, for example, the Court decided that state employees did not have to be paid according to federal wage laws. The Court decided that Congress did not have the right to interfere with affairs inside state governments.

Another Republican president, elected in 1980, continued the campaign for improving states' rights. President Ronald Reagan pointed to federal programs as another way the federal government had increased its power.

In many federal programs, the federal government supplies the states with money. But in order to get the money, the states have to abide by certain federal regulations. The Reagan administration supported the idea of "block grants." In block grants, the federal government awards funds without attaching regulations. The states thus would have more freedom to spend the money as they wished.

The Reagan administration has also proposed cutting down on the federal government's regulation of business, and reducing federal health and welfare programs. These functions, Reagan believes, should be carried out by the states. The states are closer to the people.

Whether the trend of the 1970s and 1980s will continue remains to be seen. The trend has been to return some states' rights that had been reduced earlier. The general idea is that the federal government has become too large and too strong. It proposes that more power should be shared with the states.

The relationship between state and federal government will continue to be a subject of debate during your lifetime. Think about how states' rights have changed over time. Which rights should belong to states? Which ones should belong to the federal government?

As an adult, you will help decide these questions.

For Further Reading

Anderson, William. *The Nation and the States, Rivals or Partners?* Minneapolis: University of Minnesota Press, 1955.

Bailey, Thomas A. *The American Pageant.* Boston: D. C. Heath, 1956. Pp. 125–279, 356–439, 459–502.

Bennett, Walter Hartwell. *American Theories of Federalism.* University: University of Alabama Press, 1964. Pp. 91–220.

Cunliffe, Marcus. *The Nation Takes Shape.* Chicago: University of Chicago Press, 1959. Pp. 122–80.

Davidson, James West, and Lytle, Mark H. *The United States: A History of the Republic.* Englewood Cliffs, N.J.: Prentice-Hall, 1981. Pp. 652–53, 670–71.

Elazar, Daniel J. *American Federalism: A View from the States.* New York: Thomas Crowell, 1966.

Goldwin, Robert A., ed. *A Nation of States.* Chicago: Rand McNally, 1961.

Hawkins, Robert B., ed. *American Federalism: A New Partnership for the Republic.* San Francisco: Institute for Contemporary Studies, 1982. Pp. 89–110.

Hofstadter, Richard. *Great Issues in American History, from Reconstruction to the Present Day, 1864–1969.* New York: Vintage Books, 1969. Pp. 47–66.

Hofstadter, Richard; Miller, William; and Aaron, Daniel. *The United States: The History of a Republic.* Englewood Cliffs, N.J.: Prentice-Hall, 1967. Pp. 154–287, 388–411, 452–87, 542–67, 644–65.

Mason, Alpheus Thomas. *The States Rights Debate.* Englewood Cliffs, N.J.: Prentice-Hall, 1964.

Van Deusen, Glyndon. *The Jacksonian Era.* New York: Harper & Row, 1959. Pp. 39–46, 70–71.

Index

Adams, John, 21, 23
Alabama, 57
Alien and Sedition Acts, 22–23
Anti-Federalists, 21, 22
Arkansas, 4–5, 57
Articles of Confederation, 6, 7, 9, 10, 12, 13, 15

Baker v. *Carr* (1964), 58
Bell, John, 36
Bill of Rights, 18–19, 45
Black Codes, 40–41, 46
Blacks, 4–5, 40–41, 43–48, 54, 56–58
  See also Slavery
Breckinridge, John C., 36

Calhoun, John C., 1–3, 32
California, 29–30, 32
Civil rights, 41, 45–48, 54, 56–58
Civil War, 38
Clay, Henry, 30, 31
Compromise of 1850, 30, 32
Confederate States of America, 38
Constitution, the U.S., 15–16, 18–20
Constitutional Convention, 13, 15–16, 18–20
Continental Congress, 6–7

Declaration of Independence, 6, 22
Desegregation, 4–5, 56–57
District of Columbia, 30, 32

Douglas, Stephen A., 30, 33–36
Draft, 7, 10
Dred Scott decision, 33, 35
Due process, right to, 41, 45–46

Education, 56–57
Eighteenth Amendment to the Constitution, 50
Eisenhower, Dwight D., 5
Electoral college, 44
Embargo Act of 1807, 24–25

Faubus, Orville, 4–5
Federalists, 21–22
Foreign affairs, 9, 24–25
Fort Sumter, 37, 38
Fourteenth Amendment to the Constitution, 41, 43, 45
Franklin, Benjamin, 15

Grant, Ulysses S., 44
Great Compromise, 15–16
Great Depression, 50, 52–53

Hamilton, Alexander, 15
Harlan, John Marshall, 46, 48
Hartford Convention, 25
Hayes, Rutherford B., 44
Henry, Patrick, 13, 15, 18
House of Representatives, 15–16, 44

Illinois, 33
Individual rights, 18–19, 22
Interstate Commerce Act of 1887, 49

Jackson, Andrew, 1, 3–4
Jefferson, Thomas, 6, 21–24, 27
Johnson, Andrew, 40–43
Johnson, Lyndon B., 57
Judicial review, 23–24

Kansas, 32–33
Kansas-Nebraska Act of 1854, 33
Kennedy, John F., 57
Kentucky Resolutions, 22–23

Lee, Richard Henry, 6
Lincoln, Abraham, 34–36, 38–40, 43
Little Rock, Arkansas, 4–5
Louisiana, 45
Louisiana Purchase, 27

Madison, James, 15, 18, 22–23
Maine, 28
Marbury, William, 23
Marbury v. Madison (1803), 23
Maryland, 35
Massachusetts, 10, 28
Missouri, 27, 33
Missouri Compromise of 1820, 33

Nebraska, 32–33
New Deal, 52, 53
New Hampshire, 19
New Jersey, 15
New York, 19
Nineteenth Amendment to the Constitution, 50
Ninth Amendment to the Constitution, 19
Nixon, Richard, 58–59
North Carolina, 19
Northwest Ordinance of 1787, 12
Northwest Territory, 10–12
Nullification, 23–25, 57

Parks, Rosa, 57
Plessy, Homer, 48
Political parties, 21
Poll tax, 57
Post office, 10
Prohibition, 50

Railroads, 48–49
Reagan, Ronald, 59
Reconstruction, 39–44
Republican Party, 35, 36, 40, 44
Revenue Sharing Act, 58
Rhode Island, 19
Roosevelt, Franklin D., 52, 53

Scott, Dred, 33
Secession, 25, 36, 38
Segregation, 4–5, 46–48, 56–57
Senate, 16, 18
"Separate but equal" doctrine, 48
Seventeenth Amendment to the Constitution, 50
Shays' Rebellion, 10
Sixteenth Amendment to the Constitution, 49
Slavery, 3, 11, 12, 16, 17, 27–33, 35–36, 38–40
Social Security Act, 54
South Carolina, 3–4, 36–38
States' Rights Party, 56
Supreme Court of the United States, 23, 33, 35, 46, 48, 49, 54, 56–59

Taney, Roger B., 33, 34
Tariffs, 3–4, 16
Taxation, 7, 9, 16, 49
Tenth Amendment to the Constitution, 19
Thirteenth Amendment to the Constitution, 40
Trade regulation, 9, 49
Treaties, 9–10, 18
Truman, Harry S., 54–56
Twenty-first Amendment to the Constitution, 50
Twenty-fourth Amendment to the Constitution, 57

Virginia, 15, 18, 19
Virginia Resolutions, 22–23
Voting, 9, 41, 43, 50, 51, 57

War of 1812, 24–27
Washington, George, 7, 8, 14, 15, 18, 21
Webster, Daniel, 30